Make Money Blogging:

How To Make Five-Figures Per Month Fast

By

Julie Rausch

© Copyright 2016 by JRpublishing Group All rights reserved.

The following eBook is reproduced below with the goal of providing information that is as accurate and reliable as possible. Regardless, purchasing this eBook can be seen as consent to the fact that both the publisher and the author of this book are in no way experts on the topics discussed within and that any recommendations or suggestions that are made herein are for entertainment purposes only. Professionals should be consulted as needed prior to undertaking any of the action endorsed herein.

This declaration is deemed fair and valid by both the American Bar Association and the Committee of Publishers Association and is legally binding throughout the United States.

Furthermore, the transmission, duplication or reproduction of any of the following work including specific information will be considered an illegal act irrespective of if it is done electronically or in print. This extends to creating a secondary or tertiary copy of the work or a recorded copy and is only allowed with express written consent from the Publisher. All additional rights reserved.

The information in the following pages is broadly considered to be a truthful and accurate account of facts and as such any inattention, use or misuse of the information in question by the reader will render any resulting actions solely under their purview. There are no scenarios in which the publisher or the original author of this work can be in any fashion deemed liable for any hardship or damages that may befall them after undertaking information described herein.

Additionally, the information in the following pages is intended only for informational purposes and should thus be thought of as universal. As befitting its nature, it is presented without assurance regarding its prolonged validity or interim quality. Trademarks that are mentioned are done without written consent and can in no way be considered an endorsement from the trademark holder.

CONTENTS

Introduction 1
Chapter One: Introduction to Blogging 3
Chapter Two: Popular Blog Topics & Niches 11
Chapter Three: How to Choose a Host 25
Chapter Four: How to Make Big Money Blogging 32
Chapter Five: Selling on Your Blog 44
Chapter Six: How to Market Your Blog 51
Chapter Seven: Affiliate Marketing Strategies 63
Chapter Eight: Tips, Advice, and Mistakes to Avoid 68
Conclusion 76

For **Free Offer** please visit:
http://eepurl.com/diLEWT

Introduction

The following chapters will discuss blogging and how you can make money as a blogger. You will learn what blogging is and how you can become an accomplished blogger if you have passion, apply the right tactics, and follow the simple advice.

Did you know that making a lot of money with your blog is not a pipedream? It is possible to earn a five-figure income each month just from your blog. However, you will not only have to work hard but also work smart. You will learn about the best strategies to adapt to earn an attractive income regularly.

This book discusses many relevant topics in great detail. There are topics that discuss the most profitable topics to write, how to choose a website host, and the best content management systems to use. You will learn about the most lucrative ways of monetizing your blog so that within a short time, you will be earning an income that others can only dream of.

The book also discusses many other essential topics including how to market your blog, about affiliate marketing, using applications and plugins that will boost your blog online, and so much more.

There are plenty of books on this subject on the market, thanks again for choosing this one! Every effort was made to ensure it is full of as much useful information as possible. Please enjoy!

Chapter One:

Introduction to Blogging

You have probably heard about blogging. You may even have watched a movie based on a blog. However, a lot of people are not really sure what a blog is. The term "Blog" is an abbreviated version of the word weblog.

A weblog can be described as a website that maintains an ongoing chronicle of information. It is a diary-type commentary with articles and links to other websites. However, today's weblogs are a lot more than chronicles. This is why a blog is also defined as an interface that you can use to publish content on the internet. Blogs can be used to publish news and reviews as well as discussing ideas and products.

If you spend a lot of time online, then you have probably read a blog even if you didn't realize it at the time. Most of these blogs are a lot like online magazines because they are written by a team of writers who are paid to update the blog and add fresh content a couple of times a day or week. Even then, a majority of blogs are written by an individual writer who often happens to be the blog owner. This is why most blogs are fairly personal and tend to reflect the interest and personality of the individual writer.

What Do Blogs Discuss?

Blogs discuss a wide variety of topics and subjects. These include topics such as home staging, sports, mobile technology, politics, hobbies, beauty, and so much more. Some blogs are more eclectic while others are personal journals, presenting an author's opinion, life, and thoughts. There are a couple of things that most, if not all, blogs have in common. These are articulated below:

- The main content area where articles are listed in chronological order. Latest articles are always on top. Articles are usually organized in categories.
- There is often an archive of older articles.
- Blogs often provide a comment section so that readers can write their views and contribute to the discussion.
- You are likely to see a number of links to related content and blogs.
- There will be one or more "feeds" like RSS, RDF, or Atom.

Who is a Blogger?

A blogger is any person who owns, maintains, or runs a blog. This person posts new articles on a regular basis and adds content such as video and images. Posts can also include opinions, case studies, general information, and so much more.

Generally, a good blog is one that provides useful, free information and one that helps readers stay informed on a subject of their interest. There are blogs on the internet on almost every issue imaginable. It is estimated that there are over 150 million blogs floating around the internet. Some of them focus on one topic while others discuss a variety of topics. A lot of these are self-maintained which means the owner manages their own blog. However, a number of other blogs are managed by a host of different writers.

Reasons Why Blogging is a Great Idea

Blogging can be immensely valuable to you for a variety of reasons. Numerous blog writers have benefitted personally, professionally, and financial from blogging. Many bloggers enjoy writing, and the art has become a favorite hobby. A lot of them have given up full-time jobs to focus on blogging. It gives them peace of mind, an income they could only previously dream of, and a lifestyle they have always wanted. Here are a number of reasons why you should start blogging immediately.

You attract enthusiastic readers to your blog:

As a blogger, you can reach the billions of people from around the world who use the internet regularly. Blogging attracts an audience because it provides something of value to them, yet they ask for nothing in return. If you create a blog that adds value to people's lives, then you can attract an audience which you can later convert into friends, partners, loyal customers, or anything else you want.

Establish authority:

If you own a blog and focus on writing about important topics that are relevant to your audience, then you will sooner or later establish yourself as an authority on that subject. Being an authority on a given subject enhances your professional image. In fact, a blog to a professional today is what a business card used to be in the 1990s. Blogs present you as an expert and authority in your chosen field.

Create opportunities for yourself:

Blogging can lead to traffic generating or business opportunities. For instance, you can get speaking engagements or press appearances and similar invites. Blogging enables anyone with something interesting or valuable to say to be identified as an expert; lots of bloggers have been called experts simply because they write blogs worth reading.

Organize your thoughts and learn:

As a blogger, you will have to learn a lot about what you do not know and to articulate what you know. When you begin writing a blog post, you will need to organize your thoughts. Should there be any gaps in your article, you will have to learn about it. Writing down and articulating your thoughts are great ways of internalizing something you have experienced or leaned. It also helps you become more familiar with the topic you are writing about.

Get a chance to tell your story:

As a blogger, you get to be your own media company. You can tell your own story the way you want to tell it without being dependent on journalists. It is easy to portray a story the way you want when you are the writer. You get to choose the topic and decide what information to include or leave out just as long as the blog is factual.

Get to meet new people:

You audience does not just have to remain an anonymous audience. They can become your friends, partners, associates, or even colleagues. A lot of bloggers boast of friends and even business partners who were once their readers.

Blogging gives you a chance to stand out:

Consider the fact that of all internet users, only 1% create content and the other 99% are content consumers. By blogging, you separate yourself from the 99% of people that do not blog. Standing out is essential in an increasingly competitive world.

You can make money blogging:

If you have a blog with a lot of readers, then you can monetize it and earn a regular income. In today's world, being diversified and having additional sources of income can be absolutely beneficial. If you are working a job that does not pay you much, then you could supplement your income with blogging.

Income from blogging is largely passive because it can be automated and is not directly dependent on the hours you put in. You could easily earn a five-figure income monthly through your blog. This is very possible if you focus, adapt the right approach, and put in the time.

Things a Blogger Needs to Know

As a blogger, you need to understand how your specific blogging software works. This is so that you can add content, refresh articles, and add video and photos. In addition to these, there are some concepts and terms you need to become familiar with.

Archives: A blog provides an excellent way of keeping track of articles on a site. A lot of blogs have an archive section based on dates, such as monthly or yearly archives. The front page of the blog often features a calendar of dates that are linked to daily archives. Archives can also be based on categories featuring all the related articles. You can also archive your posts alphabetically or by author.

Feeds: A Feed is a function of special software that allows sites to be accessed by "Feedreaders" searching for new content. Updates from the Feeds are then posted as updates on other sites. They provide a means for users to keep up with the hottest and latest information posted on different blogging websites. Examples of Feeds include RSS (Rich Site Summary or Really Simple Syndication), Atom or RDF files, and so on.

Syndication: A feed is simply any machine-readable content publication (often XML) that is regularly updated. Most blogs publish a feed such as RSS. Tools such as feed-readers keep checking specified blogs for updates, and when they find updates, they display the new post and link an excerpt of the post. You can have new items downloaded for you to read, so you do not have to visit all the blogs you are interested in. Simply add the link to the RSS feed of all the blogs you are interested in and you will be informed when any of these blogs have new posts in them.

Manage the comments: Many blog readers love to interact with the writer and other readers, exchanging views, and discussing interesting points. As a blog writer, you should enable comments on your website. Comments provide a highly interactive forum. Recommendations and comments made by your readers are also known as pingbacks and trackbacks.

For a long time, comments on blogs have been viewed with suspicion as they lack authority. Blog readers are sometimes anonymous and can use any name to leave a comment. Trackbacks and pingbacks both aim to provide some verification to blog commenting.

Chapter Two:
Popular Blog Topics & Niches

As a blogger, you will often be advised to blog about a topic or niche you are passionate about. While there is some truth to this statement, the best advice would be to tell you about the best niches you should consider. This is if you really want a large audience, be influential, and earn a lot of money.

If you are to be a successful blogger, then you should think about blogging with a purpose. This increases your market share, revenue growth, consumer engagement, and of course, a return on your investment. Blogging with a purpose applies whether you operate a business or not. The aim here is to be a successful blogger.

Problem Choosing Niches

There is a problem that many bloggers face and this is choosing the wrong niche for your blog. There are a number of reasons why a particular niche could be wrong for you.

Passion: It could be that you are not passionate enough about a particular niche or topic. Perhaps you do not understand it well enough, or it could be a difficult one. Plenty of people have spent a lot of money and time blogging the wrong niche only to realize this about a year or so later.

Money: Some bloggers set out to simply make money. Such a blogger picks a niche they believe will make them a lot of money. A couple of months or years later, they realize they have no zeal or passion for the niche, and so they begin losing followers. Basically, when your heart is not into something, your audience will realize, and they will start leaving in droves.

You also could be passionate about a niche, but then blogging does not make you any money. While having passion is great, making money is equally important. The financial strain that may result when you don't make any money could lead to serious challenges, and you may eventually be forced to quit blogging.

As a blogger, you need sufficient passion and drive to keep going. You also need to be able to earn plenty of money from your blog to provide you with the financial freedom that you always wanted. There are a good number of people who are earning six-figure incomes annually merely from blogging. There is no reason why this should not be you.

Chances are that the decision of which niche to blog about could affect the next five to ten years of your life especially if you are in it for the long haul. To be successful, you have to take every little factor into account.

Questions You Need to Ask Before Getting Started

What are you passionate about? This is the most important question to ask yourself. If you have no passion for a topic, then simply do not write, or blog, about it. Passion is an essential ingredient for successful blogging. It will keep you motivated and will prevent you from giving up.

You will be able to develop your skill sets in a particular niche if you are passionate about it. Another reason why passion is important is that if it is lacking, then your readers will pick up on it. And if you do not care, your readers will take off.

Is your preferred niche profitable? It is important to consider the financial benefit your blog could bring. While a lot of people blog because it is something they enjoy doing, it should be profitable as well, for long-term sustainability.

Also, consider the fact that it can take quite a while before your blog starts earning you an income. Some of the things you need to keep in mind when you ask this question include your resources, ease of attracting advertisers, whether others are making money in this niche, and what the competition is like. You can use search engines such as Google to find competitors in your niche.

If you want to earn a decent income regularly through your blog, then you need to truly understand whether you can make lots of money in your preferred niche. It is just not worth it spending the next 12 months trying to make money and failing eventually.

Is your niche viable? The truth is that some niches are too small to be viable and growth will eventually climax at a point. From thereon it will be a struggle to increase your traffic, and you will probably run out of content ideas. When considering a niche, you may want to use some keyword tools to get an idea of how many people are searching a particular keyword.

Some of the keyword research tools that you can use include Google Keyword Planner, Long Tail Pro, and SEM Rush. Even then, the figures you obtain are merely estimates that will guide you in arriving at a decision. Also look at the competition.

If your niche has competition, then it probably is a worthwhile niche. However, if the competition is quite strong and able, then you could run into difficulty because competition may just be too strong.

What does the public really need? It is important that you consider factors such as the importance of your niche to the general public, or specifically, your readers. People have different needs, and according to Maslow's Hierarchy of Needs, there are some needs that are definitely more important than others. For instance, food and water are basic needs which are essential. Video games, on the other hand, are only optional.

Do you need some niche ideas? If you need to get ideas about your blog, then you can find plenty of blogs with ideas. Consider checking out Amazon Best Seller list.

Amazon is one of the most trusted retailers in the world, and this is why simply recommending a product on Amazon can lead to more people purchasing it. The Amazon bestseller list covers all categories that there are. Categories include hot new releases, top rated, and many others.

Niche Research Tools

Long Tail Pro: This is a search tool that allows you to add as many seed keywords as possible. It provides you with filters that enable you to identify the most appropriate keywords.

SEM rush: This is another popular tool used by many experts, including bloggers. You can use it to find inspiring blog post ideas. You also get to learn about your competitors, what keywords are common and how the competition ranks.

Google Keyword Planner: This is an extension of Google Adwords which allows bloggers to perform keyword research on the fly. It is the replacement for the Keyword External Tool and works great for writers and bloggers. Profit is however not found in passion but in popularity.

Identify Blogging Topics That Will Make You Money

According to experienced bloggers, it is possible to make money in almost any niche that you decide to enter. However, you should also know that some niches are a lot easier to build an audience and make money with than others. Your goal should be to follow your passion while earning a great income.

The best place to start is to identify a problem rather than a niche. Being able to identify a problem and then addressing the problem is an even better approach. Of course, if you take a step back, you will realize that the problem falls into a niche but identifying a problem provides a far better approach. A lot of the time, bloggers pick on a niche then write about it until they encounter a problem that resonates with people. Also note that, once you start making money with something, you will become passionate about it.

What Do People Want?

You really need to understand what it is that people want. Generally, people need a problem solved. Simply put, most people want a better version of themselves or they want to make their lives easier. For instance, if you promise to show them how to become a better parent, how to manage their finances better, or even how to get the body they want, then they will listen. In other words, niches that show people how to be better versions of themselves are the niches that you want to enter.

Best Niches to Start a Blog

1. How to make money: This may sound like an obvious niche, but it is actually the elephant in the room. If you want a profitable blog, then teach people about how to make money. However, it can be a tricky niche if you are not actually making money. Readers are not easily fooled. You have to show them that you really know what you are talking about.

So if you want to start blogging on this topic but have no prior experience, then you can consider a secondary blog. Some of the well-known bloggers in this niche include Amy Lynn Andrews, Melyssa Griffin, Darren Rowse, and John Lee Dumas among others.

2. Personal Finance: Personal finance is different from how to make money as the focus is more on savings and investing rather than earning. Some personal finance sites teach readers how to save their money through frugal living. Others teach you how to invest your money and side jobs you can take to boost your finances. Take Michelle Gardner for instance. She is a leading blogger in this niche and earns most of her income through an affiliate link and an affiliate marketing course. Niche areas are very important. You stand a better chance of success with niche areas than general writing.

3. Health and Fitness: This is another great area that can bring a lot of traffic to your blog. However, you need to really understand the sector if you are to monetize it. The best approach is to get into affiliate marketing. This is because your audience is seeking solutions to a problem. A nice link to a product on sites such as Amazon is a recommendation they would appreciate, especially from an expert on the topic. Plenty of blogs in this niche are often run by teams of experts such as fitness trainers, dieticians, and others.

4. Food: While food sounds simple enough, it can be quite tricky because your audience will be largely looking for recipes rather than things to buy. You can still proceed with this topic and aim to build a large enough audience. You may want to look at blogs like Food Blogger Pro. This blog teaches how to start a food blog in smaller niches. You can also use ads on your website to bring in additional income.

5. Fashion and Beauty: This is an excellent niche because you will not only sell great products but will also gain access to cool events. However, this niche relies more on your personality and getting out there. This means showing videos, displaying photos, and attending events. However, a lot of written content is also essential.

Many beauty and fashion bloggers focus more on social networking sites such as Instagram and YouTube because they are visual platforms. It is after they gather a substantial following that they begin blogging. Even then, most of these blogs end up becoming lifestyle blogs covering a variety of topics in fashion and beauty.

6. Lifestyle: This is a very broad topic, and you may need to search for a sub-niche within the niche. Some of the sub-niches include gardening, outdoor décor, travel, home, survival, among numerous others. These are just some of the more prominent ones. If you focus on one of these, then you stand a better chance of monetizing your blog. Monetization methods for this niche are more often printable or ads. Topics like gardening, the homestead, and survival are really big, and you can never go wrong with these.

7. Personal development: Personal development can be a tricky subject mostly because bloggers do not focus on a specific problem and tend to generalize the niche. It is a major blunder to be vague and write generally about living a better life. With this niche, you need to be specific about exactly what issues you are targeting and the types of solutions you are offering. For instance, you can help your readers get rid of bad habits such as procrastination or conditions like depression.

Types of Articles to Write

Even after you identify your preferred niche, there are still other decisions to make regarding content. If you own or manage a brand, then you need to understand your customers, topics that are important to them and the products or services you are selling. But if you are an individual blogger, then you should identify a topic that will captivate your audience. There are different article types and topics that you can consider. Here is a look at some of them.

1. Listicles: Listicles are simply articles made up of lists. Marketers are not fond of listicles, but they consist some of the most popular articles on the internet. They are used by firms such as Buzzfeed and are favored even by the New York Times. A listicle is ultimately an article whose core is a list of items.

Good examples of listicle articles include, "5 Things You Need to Know About London" or "6 Ways to Earn an Extra Income." Many like listicles because they are highly visual, trendy, fun, brief in nature, and shareable. However, there are some disadvantages of these kinds of articles. For instance, they are unprofessional, un-original, spammy, and basically not very informative. The bottom line is, people love reading listicles. It is not just a trend but a proven fact.

2. How to Articles: People generally abhor reading instruction manuals. It is not easy to find anyone snuggled up with a glass of wine reading an instruction manual. Consumers mostly use search engines such as Google to figure out how to do stuff. One particular blog has become very popular for its how-to articles. If you can identify your niche audience and cater to their curiosities, then you can come up with an excellent blog that will very likely be popular with readers.

3. Write about Politics: People love reading about politics especially during election years. They enjoy reading both national and local politics and possibly even join the conversation. Politics can be dicey. It can polarize people so be prepared to handle some controversy especially if you take sides and not present

4. Ultimate Guides: Many subject matter experts are always seeking out the most credible ultimate guides for their area of expertise. The term "ultimate guide," though, is overused so you can find alternative terms if you like. For instance, you can write an Essential Guide, Complete Guide, Uncensored Guide, and so on.

5. Frequently Asked Questions: You can also write about frequently asked questions. You need to understand, though, that even when you post answers to frequently asked questions online, people will still keep asking questions anyway. Frequently asked questions serve as a resource for people and are often featured on e-commerce websites but overlooked on blogs. FAQs are popular on Google's algorithms and with people of all ages.

6. Product Reviews: Basically, product reviews are a trusted online resource for information, and they tend to draw traffic to blogs and websites. They are also an attractive revenue stream for bloggers. If you are considering monetizing your blog instantly, then product reviews will get you there. What you need to do is link to product pages through affiliate links like Amazon Affiliates. You will be able to monetize your blog almost entirely. You need to ensure that you choose a specific niche as this will provide a platform for expertise and credibility.

Here Are a Couple of Other Topics that You Can Write About

- Sourced news
- Gifs and memes

- People features
- Personal stories
- Interviews
- Beginner guides
- Recipes

Remember that popular topics come and go. You might pick a technique today, and it runs out of favor tomorrow. This is part of the excitement and drama that is blogging. Simply deal with it, gather your traffic and move on. The topics listed above are virtually guaranteed to make you a top blogger in your niche and earn you lots of money.

Chapter Three:

How to Choose a Host

Now that you are ready to set up your blog, you need to identify an appropriate host who will provide you with excellent blog hosting services that you require. There are several types of blog hosts but how do you decide which blog host is best for you? It is advisable to first find out what is available out there and then make a decision based on that.

Factors to Consider When Choosing a Host

1. *Cost*: The cost of hosting a blog is important and depends on the services your host is providing. You should review the services offered by several blog hosts and find out the one that matches your needs at the most affordable price. You may then do some research or ask other bloggers what host they currently use. This will give you some insights into current services and prices.

2. *Look at data transfer limitations:* Ensure that you check how much data you are allowed to transfer to your blog each month when reviewing different hosts. There is a transfer limit, and this needs to be high enough to accommodate all your data needs. Remember that you can always upgrade to higher transfer limits as your blog grows, so do not initially overbuy.

3. Check reliability of speed and uptime: It is extremely important to understand the uptime offered by your blog host. Generally, if visitors can't view your blog or you are unable to log in and update information, then there isn't much point in visiting it again. Also, if the speed in accessing your blog is too slow simply because your host's server has exceeded its capacity, your readers will become frustrated. Your host really needs to be reliable when it comes to speed and uptime.

4. Space allotted: As an account holder with a hosting company, you will be allocated a specific amount of server space to store your blogs. You need to check and confirm the space allocation for the different hosting packages on offer. This will enable you to select the best option for your needs and budget. As a blogger, you will not need terabytes of space so do not fall for costly packages that offer large amounts of space.

5. ***Support provided***: As a blogger, you may require assistance, advice, and support from time to time. If you have a question or a problem about your hosting services, it is important that your blog host has a support team available at all times to assist you. Review the type of support available before eventually making a decision.

Hosting Options

WordPress: WordPress is a popular blog hosting site and provides free services to any interested blogger. The website www.wordpress.com stores your site's content for free on its servers. However, you receive a very limited version of the software. Yet it is still a very nice host and the choice of millions of bloggers from around the world. It is also a great website for those who wish to upgrade to a self-hosted WordPress blog at a future date. WordPress is favored because it has no set-up costs, is simple to use with no coding or design knowledge necessary and comes with hundreds of themes to choose from. However, WordPress looks less professional, comes with limited functionality and you basically do not own your blog. Your blog also comes with a .wordpress domain.

Blogger: Since Blogger is owned by Google, you will receive access to plenty of Google tools such as Analytics and AdSense. The problem is that Blogger is not as flexible as WordPress. It is great for brand builders and hobby bloggers who have no desire to invest any money but wish to make some cash through ads. It is quite easy to use and is a good place for beginners to start learning the ropes. Some benefits include the fact that it is completely free to use, can access HTML code and you can place AdSense ads. Main challenges are there are fewer themes to choose from, smaller storage space, your blog comes with a .blogspot tag in the title and you cannot self-host.

Tumblr: This platform is easy to use and is a truly social platform. It is ideal for bloggers who like the idea of "re-blogging" posts from elsewhere on the web. It has a platform that is suitable for micro-bloggers, so it might not be the perfect place for those seeking a platform for long-form content. Major benefits include unlimited storage, thousands of themes to choose from, and HTML, CSS access for customization. The downside includes difficulty backing up blog and importing content, limited plugin options, and very difficult to monetize.

TypePad: This is a paid platform that costs less than $10 per month. It provides an excellent platform for brand builders and business professionals who don't mind investing some cash every month into their blog. The fee you pay each month can translate into more and better features with a professional-looking blog. Even then, experts advise business owners to opt for

WordPress due to its large community. TypePad has advantages such as you own your blog, the platform is easy to use, and you get unlimited storage space. The issues you may encounter are limited customization options and higher costs than a self-hosted WordPress site.

WIX: This is another paid platform that costs less than $5 per month. It is a great website hosting option that comes with excellent blogging features and is ideal for business owners. WIX makes building your entire e-commerce website simple even though full control over your e-commerce site is sort of limited. The pros include unlimited bandwidth, ease of use, ad integration, domain registration options, hundreds of professional-looking templates, and 20 GB storage space.

Free vs. Paid Blog Hosting

Free hosted blog: This is a blog that is hosted at no cost to the blogger and the one that most people turn to when they want to start blogging. All you need to do is visit your preferred host, sign up for an account and begin blogging almost immediately. They include Live Journal, Tumblr, WordPress.com and a few others.

Pros and cons of free blog hosting: They are great for newbies and those just starting to blog. Tumblr, for instance, allows re-blogging other people's posts. However, they do have limitations such as limited functionality, limited space and so on.

Pros and cons of self-hosting: Some sites such as WordPress are very popular with millions of users. WordPress uses open source code, allowing thousands of coders from around the world to improve the sites for free. Using such self-blogging sites is very easy with thousands of free plugins and themes. The only downside is the monthly cost that you incur for the service.

WordPress and Bluehost

There are more than 2 million people around the world who use Bluehost to host their blogs. Bloggers using Bluehost are more likely to succeed compared to those on free hosts and free blogging platforms.

You can use WordPress on Bluehost very easily. It takes only a couple of clicks to set it up. WordPress recommends Bluehost to bloggers. You get to enjoy the full benefits of WordPress, including all features, add-ons, themes, and plugins. Hosting your own blog on Bluehost is really affordable. All that you require is a domain name and a hosting package that costs about $2.75 per month.

Bluehost provides you with services such as 24-hour live chat support, one-click WordPress installation, your very own domain name, unlimited blogs and domain names, and personalized email addresses. The security of your blog is enhanced while you enjoy excellent uptime almost 99% of the time. You also get a chance to choose from different blogging platforms and access to various free programs and software. Bluehost and WordPress come highly recommended by bloggers around the world.

Chapter Four:

How to Make Big Money Blogging

Now that you know how to start a blog, the next step should be how to monetize it. There are bloggers who own multiple blogs with each earning about $1 million every year. While this may be an exception, it is very possible to earn a very attractive income regularly by blogging. You can make big money blogging whether it's a business blog or a hobby blog.

First of all, you should understand that it is not an easy process. It does take some hard work so be prepared to put in the work initially. Also, blogging is not a get rich quick scheme. However, if you do it right, you could make enough money to improve your lifestyle and support your family and more. The moment you decide to start using your blog to make money, you are no longer just a blogger. You also become an entrepreneur and your blog a small business.

How Blogs Make Money

- Blogs attract visitors with free content

- They offer readers a freebie in exchange for their email addresses
- Blogs then build trust by consistently providing useful content
- Bloggers should offer a product or service that will genuinely help the readers
- Once trust is established, bloggers sell different products and services to readers on a regular basis

Apparently, if you are to make money through your blog, then you should use it as a lead generation mechanism. Nurture those leads until they are ready to purchase, and the profits will start pouring in. This is a process that could take months or even years, so learn to be patient.

You can start a blog, or two, and work on them at night and on the weekends. You can also work on them at any other time when you are free. Sometimes blogging involves putting in hundreds of hours into research, content, and writing. It can also cost you hundreds, if not thousands, of dollars. As a determined blogger with a desire to provide useful information and eventually start making money, you should persevere and continue learning. Liaise with other bloggers and learn their tactics, approaches, and tips that they have successfully deployed.

Create Useful Content

A blog is not a blog without content, so once you've set up your blog, your focus should be on creating useful content. Your content will largely depend on your preferred niche and the topics you choose to write about. Most of the successful bloggers focus on niches or a certain demographic that they write for.

The key to successful content creation is making it as useful as possible. You should focus on creating content that changes people's lives in one way or another. This will make them feel like they know you and can trust you. This is really important if you are to make money from your blog.

Keep track of metrics: You need to know the number of people visiting your blog each day, each week, each month, and so on. Metrics are important. Your blog could be highly valued if it starts to receive about 1000 visitors per day. There are bloggers who have been known to sell their blogs for thousands of dollars once they attain such readership. You may not want this approach because a blog can earn you a large income each month for many years to come.

Use the Content to Build Credibility

When you start out, you should blog to build credibility. Credibility will help lead to more money-making opportunities. For instance, if you start blogging in the finance industry, people will start reading your content, and shortly thereafter, your blog will become very popular. Soon you become a recognized figure in the finance industry.

Once you become such an authority figure in the field of finance, others will start approaching you with offers like help to co-write a book on debt management or an invite to speak to a group of employees on personal finances. Many bloggers have built a name this way. You, too, can build a name for yourself and start receiving offers once you establish yourself as an authority.

Remember that as a blogger, you shouldn't just put up a blog and let it stay there. A blog has to be dynamic. You have to provide fresh content on a regular basis. You also have to engage with your readers, interact with them especially through the comment section. It might take some time before you get significant following, but you have to keep working towards it. If you put in the time and hard work, it will definitely pay off in due course of time.

Make Money with Advertisements

One of the most common ways that bloggers make money is through ads placed on their sites. There are basically two types of such ads. These are CPC and CPM.

CPC or PPC ads: Cost per Click or Pay per Click ads are often banners placed in your content or sidebar. Each time a visitor to your blog clicks on the ads, you get paid for the click.

CPM ads: CPM ads are also known as "Cost per 1000 Impressions" ads. These ads pay you a fixed amount of money based on how many people view the advertisement.

The most common network for placing these types of ads is known as Google AdSense. This is a program from Google that provides you with an opportunity to make money online by placing ads on your website. You are essentially turning your blogging passion into profit.

Almost 2 million people around the world have chosen to use Google AdSense on their websites. AdSense can carefully select the right ads for your audience. All ads are reviewed to ensure they are high quality and relevant to your readers. It keeps you in control of the ad process because you can remove or block ads you do not like and choose which types fit your blog best. You also customize sections where ads appear. AdSense only lets highest paid ads go live on your website.

Getting Started With AdSense

The first step is to get your website up and running. You cannot join AdSense until your website is well established. While it doesn't need to have thousands of followers and hundreds of monthly views each month, there are a few basic requirements. You will require at least a blog or website that has a decent amount of richly written, text-based content with reasonably good traffic and should be at least 3 months old.

The website need not necessarily be yours, but you should at least be able to access and make changes to the source code for its pages so that you can coordinate where to post your ads on the pages. Even then, it is strongly recommended that you have your own website. Also, your site should not link to adult content or material that infringes copyright and should not be spammy in any way.

Now once your website has met the basic criteria, you can apply for and register a Google AdSense account. This is again a fairly easy process. If you have an existing Google account, you can use it. If you do not have one, you should consider opening one. It is really easy and takes only a couple of seconds to do so.

Once the application process is complete, you should proceed to your account and answer a few questions about your blog. AdSense will ask you questions about your site's language, its content, URL, and similar questions. You will then have to sign the terms and conditions page and fill in their form providing your contact information and so on. Then you will wait for 48 hours and see if you got approved.

But you should not be limited to AdSense only because there are numerous other programs that offer similar services. They include Infolinks, Chitika, and Media.net. You do not need to be in direct contact with advertisers as all these details are taken care of. All you need to do is select where the ads should be on your blog.

Make Money Selling Private Ads

You can also make money by selling private ads to willing buyers. You do not need to limit yourself to advertising networks like AdSense and others. If your blog starts attracting a sizeable traffic, advertisers will come trooping and ask to put ads on your blog. Alternatively, you can contact advertisers directly. The best part of it all is that you do not need to go through middlemen.

By eliminating middlemen, you get to state your own ad rates. This will definitely translate into more money. You can sell private ads through banners, links, and buttons. You can also earn money writing sponsored posts where you write about or give a review of an advertiser's product or service. There are plenty of firms and businesses that need bloggers to promote their content for marketing purposes. Another variation to this option is to write a series of posts on any topic, but the advertiser pays for it. In return, you simply state that the information is "Brought to you by"; mention in the content.

You can use other different approaches such as charging a one-time fee to insert a link to a post. If you choose to host a banner or banner ads, you could then opt to charge your clients a fixed monthly fee.

Sponsored posts and banner ads provide great ways of generating revenue. Depending on your following, you could charge anything from $50 to $500 for sponsored articles. As a blogger, it is important that you clearly declare when a blog post is an advertisement because there are rules in some countries that govern sponsored posts.

You can also have companies sponsor an entire blog if you are publishing content within their niche. Many companies are happy to sponsor a blog and pay good money for it. However, you will have to mention the company by name on the blog. Sometimes you have to mention the company name in the header or sidebar, depending on what you agree with the client.

Opt for Recurring Income

Yet another growing category of income that more and more bloggers are using is recurring income streams. These particular ones are also known as membership programs or continuity programs.

You will need to organize your blog such that readers have to pay a recurring amount on an annual or monthly basis for access to a community area or premium content. It could also be access to some kind of service, coaching, or useful tools that will add value to their lives or work.

Incorporate a Jobs Board

You could make an additional income by advertising vacant positions on your blog. ProBlogger.net does this very well. If you have a decent number of followers, you can offer your visitors or anyone else to post vacancies on your blog. Just ensure that these are genuine positions offered by genuine individuals or credible businesses. You can then charge them a fee, like $50 per job post for a week.

Add Affiliate Links to your Content

As a blogger, you can include affiliate links to the content on your blog. It is a great way of monetizing your blog. Basically, an advertiser has a product that he or she wants to sell. The advertiser agrees to pay you a commission for each sale if a buyer originates from your blog.

The advertiser will provide you with a unique link that tracks your affiliate code. That way, she knows when a buyer used your link to make a purchase. You then include this link on your site. This is easily achieved directly through content. You can also use banners if you so wish. If one of your readers clicks on your unique links and buys the product you have recommended, then you earn a percentage of what the customer purchased.

Affiliate marketing is an entire topic on its own and shall be discussed in greater detail in a different chapter. You can make use of affiliate marketing opportunities through ad networks such as Amazon Associates or create a private partnership with businesses that have affiliate programs and advertisers.

Consider Doing Webinars

Once you have a sufficiently large following, you should collect email addresses then on occasion, invite members to a webinar. You need to prepare a very informative and presentable webinar that will add value to the lives of your followers.

Many experienced bloggers make serious money with webinars. Take Jon Morrow, an established blogger, and writer. Jon claims to make about $60,000 from just a single webinar, by inviting his followers. He charges about $20 per head and gets a viewership of 3000 or more. His topics are rather catchy though, like "How to make $500 per guest post". Your readers really appreciate quality and will be willing to pay for all quality products you offer. In fact, Jon Morrow makes most of his income from webinars such as the one described above.

Just remember, it is never too early to start monetizing your blog/website. Experts advise bloggers to start selling on day one. Do not wait until you attain a certain number of views or maybe gain 1000 followers and so on. Start earning as soon as possible. Do not lose an opportunity to make money on your blog.

Hold or Host Events

There are plenty of bloggers who also make money by hosting events. There are a number of events that you can host. They include conferences, seminars, sales meetings, meet-ups, and tons of others. Take for instance the Pro-Blogger Conference that was organized by ProBlogger.net, (a blog that focuses on online work, gigs, and blogging). The conference hosts hundreds of blogger each year who meet to share ideas and discuss matters crucial to the industry. Even online events and summits are popular with bloggers and their readers.

Chapter Five:

Selling on Your Blog

Selling products and services on your blog is one of the absolute best ways to turn loyal customers into a consistent revenue stream. In fact, a lot of bloggers set out with the hope of eventually selling products or services to the public. Selling can be a really simple process if you put your mind to it.

Factors that determine how successful you will be selling on your blog are your audience and conversion rate. The size of your audience is an important factor, and so is the number that you can convert into actual customers.

How to Increase Your Conversion Rate

As a blogger, you should first focus on building a substantial following. This has already been previously discussed at length. Now you need to focus on converting your readers into customers. You do this by presenting a real value proposition with the products or services you are selling. Even if you create engaging, shareable content that your readers treasure, offering them a product that has little to nothing to do with what the blog is all about is a sure route to failure.

Simply said, you should try and focus on providing your clients with products or services that resonate with the content of your blog. It could be something as simple as selling an e-book that you have written or perhaps selling your professional services as a consultant within your chosen field. Whatever you sell, never forget what brings your audience to your blog in the first place.

Sell Yourself and Your Products

When you are selling products to your customers, try and show them clearly how the product will make their lives easier and more fulfilling. The fact is, most of us encounter sales pitches and advertisements each day. Customers have learned to shut their ears to adverts that over-promise and underdeliver.

However, due to your blog, and your expert knowledge of the subject matter, your customers will very likely trust you. You will, therefore, have separated yourself from the pack especially if you can build a case and convince your readers of the importance and benefits of your products and services.

Sell Other People's Products on Your Blog

A great way of earning an income is through selling other people's products on your website. You can point your readers towards products being offered somewhere else, and this can be pretty lucrative for you.

Most companies will reward you for this. Rates often vary and will depend on some factors such as frequency of orders from you blog and volume of sales or any formal agreement. You could easily make up to $500 a week if you choose your niche well.

Sell Services on Your Blog

Once you become a proficient blogger, you should proceed to sell your services to interested followers. Practically everyone has a skill that businesses need. Offering your time and expertise is a great way to earn an income through your blog. Services have the highest profit margins since you are selling your time and not any physical products. If you are great at what you do, then earning $300 a week or more is very possible.

Training and Consulting: You can promote and sell your expertise to deliver training and consultancy services to businesses and even corporations. It can be a highly profitable way to create a stable, recurrent income. Bloggers often work with businesses to get started with blogging and providing marketing tips to promote their posts. You can opt for pay-per-minute phone call consulting as an additional income stream. Lots of experts make between $1000 and $2500 a week providing training and counseling per week.

Writing Services: You can also sell writing services to businesses. A lot of businesses are now writing their own blogs in the hope of engaging their audiences. As such, there is a huge demand for competent writers and bloggers. With your successful blog, you are likely to be called upon to provide these services to different businesses and organizations. Established writers can earn $200 per article or even upwards of $500 for technical and white papers.

Sell Physical Products on Your Blog

There are plenty of physical products that you can sell to your clients. They do not have to be your own. You can identify suitable products even on other websites and sell to your clients. You will get a slice of the profits when your readers buy directly from your blog.

Digital products: You can also sell digital products such as eBooks, productivity software, music, recipes, and many others. It is easy to sell such goods because there is no packaging or shipping. The amount you earn will, however, vary depending on factors such as sales volumes and so on.

Sell Membership Sites

Now if you have an active community on your blog that is hoping to learn more about your niche area, then there could be a great opportunity to come up with a paid membership area. Members would be required to pay a fee to see extra content on your site. These are mostly videos or learning resources. Take for instance internet marketer Brian Dean. He has a blog called SEOThatWorks.com. He charges members $2000 to join yet he has dozens of happy customers.

Sell Online Training Courses and eBooks

If you are already offering consulting and training services, then you could package your materials into an online course. When you offer a course in MP3 or video format, then your students could follow at their own pace. If you already have an email list of your readers, then you could easily market these courses to them. You will be surprised at how many will happily sign up to buy these products from you. Bloggers have been known to earn $800 weekly or more within their first year.

Build the Blog Sales Funnel

An important concept that is absolutely useful to bloggers is the Blog Sales Funnel. This is a marketing concept that works very well all the time. Even if you have other streams earning you money, you should definitely develop your own product down the line. There is a "funnel flow" that the process has to go through. It is very similar to a sales funnel.

First, a company entices you with a freebie. You will most likely love the freebie and feel honored by the company's actions. Next, you will be offered something rather cheap but quite irresistible. The firm will then gradually sweet talk you into buying more and more expensive things. This is a tried and tested marketing tactic that works. It is an approach that you can use for your blog.

You should adopt this strategy but in reverse. A lot of bloggers start off by trying to sell eBooks on their blogs. However, they get frustrated when they only make very little money. As a blogger, you should have other more expensive products down the line. However, start by selling the more expensive ones first then move on to cheaper and cheaper products. Think about selling products on your blog that cost $9,995, then $5,495 followed by $1,495, $545, $195, all the way down to $45. You are likely to make more money using this kind of approach.

There is No Cheap Market

It is possible to also sell products that cost $10,000 or more. Most bloggers might consider this amount way too costly for their readers. And they could be right. Out of a base of 50,000 readers, 98% may not be able to afford the product. But if you can sell the $10,000 product to 2% of your readers, you will earn a significant profit. The $10,000 product can be a year-long training program for bloggers, for instance. If you can find just 100 readers to buy the program, then that number is more than enough. Generally, you will make more money selling to the 2% than the 98%.

Chapter Six:

How to Market Your Blog

There are plenty of enthusiastic bloggers on the internet who write useful, good quality content that people want to read. However, even the best-written blog becomes useless if no one knows of its existence. According to renowned bloggers, you need to spend about 90% of your time marketing your blog compared to only 10% writing and adding content.

Fortunately, there are numerous ways of promoting and marketing your blog to potential followers. You should identify and try as many of these as possible. Below, we will take a look at some of the most important ones.

Join a Blogging Community

One of the best ways of marketing your blog is to hang out with other bloggers. You need to spend time and hang out with other bloggers to listen to their views, marketing tactics, and suggestions. By hanging out with fellow bloggers, your blog and articles will be shared within the community, and you will gain popularity very fast.

Participate in Aggregate Sites and Up-Vote Communities

Aggregate sites are places to go for information from many different sources related to a specific topic. You can share your own content on these sites to help community members with similar interests.

The up-vote aspect of these communities takes on a social role and gives the site's users the chance to like or dislike things. This provides a great way of keeping the community engaged and to weed out junk content. Examples of websites in this area include Reddit, Product Hunt, Lobsters, and Growth Hackers among others.

Use Outreach and Partnerships to Promote your Blog

You should consider sharing your blog posts with people who have shared similar content before. Basically, you should start with people who've shared similar content from your competitors. However, always ensure that the quality of your content matches or exceeds that from your competitors.

Optimize your Blog for Search Engines

One of the best ways of getting web users to find your blog is to optimize it for search engines. This is achieved through a process known as SEO or search engine optimization. The process is not as complicated as it may sound. You should start by choosing a couple of keywords to optimize your blog. You need to choose the right keywords and keyword phrases that are prominent in your niche. Use these keywords strategically within your content. Think about what people search for when using search engines to find things within your niche. Use those search terms as keywords within your content. You will draw a lot of organic traffic to your blog this way.

Use Links from Previous Content to your Current Articles

Links are very powerful when it comes to SEO. When you add links on your page that redirect readers back to previous content, your blogs will be ranked highly by search engines, and this will give you a better chance of being listed top. Search engines often look for content with links believing these to be important, so they rank them highly.

Make Use of Social Media

The evolution of media apps and expansion of social media are only going to pick up steam. Social media websites have taken off, providing bloggers with a huge arsenal of tools and resources to market themselves. You should endeavor to market your blog effectively using popular social media websites. Some of the most important ones are Twitter, Facebook, Linked, Pinterest, and Instagram among many others.

You should create different profiles on each social media website. On LinkedIn, you want to be professional and all about business. On Facebook, you should show a little of your personality while on Twitter, shine the spotlight directly onto your blog. Each social media profile should be crafted to show a different facet of your personality and expertise.

> ➤ *Marketing your Blog on Pinterest*

Pinterest is one of the best social media platforms for businesses and blog owners. This popular social media site enables bloggers to attract more visitors to their blogs. It also enables them to engage more with new and existing customers.

There are plenty of free tools available. Simply create a pin board for your blog posts then add new pins each time you add new content. Images are very powerful on this platform so find some colorful and powerful ones to use. Here are some reasons why Pinterest is preferred by bloggers.

Pinterest helps you convert more visitors into buyers: Using this powerful platform, you will easily be able to gain more visitors and customers. Visitors from Pinterest are more likely to convert faster into sales than those from other sources. Many firms turn to Pinterest for inspiration and for research.

Pinterest provides you with free tools and free analytics: As a blogger, you can add these tools to your blog and make it easier for your readers to save stuff they love and transfer it to Pinterest. There will be more of your stuff on Pinterest, and more users will be able to access it. You will also be able to see how you are engaging with your readers and what they are sharing from your website.

Pinterest drives traffic to your blog and helps increase links back to your website. Your user engagement will increase drastically, and you will find out what your audience really loves.

> *Market your Blog on Facebook*

Facebook is probably the first social network that comes to mind. It is one of the largest and most widely used social media sites. You should open a Facebook page for your blog and then introduce it to the group pages you belong to and those relevant to your niche. The best Facebook posts are those with large images and short yet clear descriptions.

➢ *Use Twitter*

Twitter is another great social network that allows you to market your blog for free. Once you write a new blog, you can market it on the site for free. You should continue marketing the blog for at least one week on Twitter but make sure to change the wording. This will prevent the spammer label being associated with your account. It will also help you reach a lot more readers. Your followers are likely to retweet your tweets and share with their followers. This will increase your reach and definitely draw more readers to your blog.

➢ *Market on LinkedIn*

It is important to market your blog on LinkedIn. This provides you with a chance to present yourself as a cultured and educated professional. You should share your blog posts on LinkedIn to receive views from other professionals in the same industry, especially those who find your work informative, interesting and relevant.

➢ *Consider Using Reddit*

Reddit is a very popular site. If you post your blog on this site, users will evaluate your content and possibly give it lots of likes. This will ensure that your content climbs up the ladder. Reddit users vote to each and every blog or content. The higher you climb due to likes, the more the people that will come and visit your blog. Check out their rules before posting because they enforce them regularly.

You Need to Use Email Marketing

Getting traffic to your blog is essential if you want to build a sizeable following. This will make your blog not just popular but also profitable. You need to start collecting emails from your visitors from your very first day and keep growing your email list. Having an email subscriber list is the fastest way to grow your readership and, eventually, your blogging income.

An email list presents one of the most direct and easiest ways of reaching readers who are most interested in your content. By accepting to receive emails from you means they interested in receiving even more from you. The reason email is so powerful as a marketing tool is that it is a very personal means of communicating. There are tools that you can use to manage your email list. A good example of these tools is Constant Contact. It is user-friendly, and you do not need to sacrifice any functionality to get a great user interface.

MailChimp

MailChimp is an excellent marketing tool that you have to use. It is often referred to as the second brain for your blog or business. It is considered an extra brain because it automatically helps you find and connect with your readers, enabling you to build with your audience so you can build your brand and also sell a lot more stuff. The best part about MailChimp is that it is free to use.

With MailChimp you get to:

- Build your brand
- Sell more stuff
- Send better emails
- Automate your marketing
- Put your data to work

AWeber is another email marketing tool that provides you with affordable and easy to use marketing and auto-responder tools. This email marketing software can greatly promote your blog and help you reach out to more readers and manage your marketing even better.

Newsletters are Effective Marketing Tools

A newsletter is an effective marketing tool because it replaces advertisements which many consumers dislike. Consumers want to know what's going on with the companies and businesses they buy from but without the ads.

Newsletter marketing is the process of sending out informational newsletters to interested parties, in this case, your readers. They offer businesses and bloggers an opportunity to connect with their loyal customers over email. Sending newsletters through email is faster and cheaper. It produces data which can be studied to create more relevant newsletters.

To successfully market using newsletters, always have a strategy. Here is a good strategy that you can employ.

- Develop reserve content and keep it aside for months.
- Read your competitor's newsletters and see what deals and articles are offered.

- Develop relationships with firms that interest readers and partner with them.
- Research your readers to know what content is best for the newsletters.
- Recycle content but reduce length and frequency. Less is always better.
- Encourage readers to give you a feedback.

Leave Comments on Relevant Blogs

You should also consider commenting on other blogs within your niche. This is an excellent marketing strategy for your blog. By reading and leaving comments on relevant blogs, you will be up-to-date with all the latest news and trends in your niche. You will also help direct traffic to your blog. You can choose to become a professional commenter and effectively build relations with other major players in your sector.

Market your Blog on StumbleUpon

The website StumbleUpon provides an excellent platform where you can find individuals with similar interests, same hobbies, education, and even jobs. You can share your posts on this platform, so you get views of your peers and people who truly understand what you are writing about. These are people who are generally interested in your article and will no doubt enable you to get more views.

Google+

Another great social media site that you cannot ignore is Google+. This is also another excellent way of getting views on your content. One advantage is that Google has millions of users. If you have a Google account, then you can invite all people on your mailing list to follow you on Google+. As you share your articles and other things on Google+, do not forget to interact with your readers and others within your circle of friends on a regular basis. Your friends and people who know you are more likely to share your content with other followers, further extending your reach and increasing your readership.

Chapter Seven:

Affiliate Marketing Strategies

Affiliate marketing is one of the most effective ways to start monetizing your blog and helping your readers at the same time. It has the capability to power your blog's residual income for a long time.

What is Affiliate Marketing?

Generally, bloggers create a following and then build trust with their readers. Thereafter, they offer them products and services that will add value to their lives. Affiliate marketing is a way of selling products and services that belong to others and getting a share of the profit. It is more like getting a commission from a sale which is really a common practice.

For bloggers, it is your duty to find the products or services you like and then promote them on your blog. You need to provide a link which your readers can use to purchase affiliate products and services. When your readers buy a product, or pay for services using your link, this is recorded, and then your commission paid out to you in due course of time.

Why is Affiliate Marketing a Great Choice for Bloggers?

As a smart blogger, you should be a fan of selling affiliate products and services. There are plenty of compelling reasons why you should consider it.

- You can easily monetize your blog much sooner than if you had to create your own blog from scratch. Earning between $50 and $100 per day is very possible.
- You will learn about the types of products your audience desires, reducing the risk of any future product launch you may undertake.
- You can get your followers and readers used to the idea of buying products and services from you. This helps increase their level of trust so long as you pick the right kind of products and services to sell.

These are impressive advantages that should excite you. There are additional benefits why this is an ideal income stream for bloggers. Here are some of the benefits of affiliate marketing.

- *Affiliate marketing is a very simple strategy to implement:* As a blogger, all you need to do is to share a link. There is no worrying about customer service, handling products, tracking sales and all that. These will be handled by the merchant.

- *You do not require any special expertise:* You do not have to be an expert even in your own niche. You simply need to be sufficiently aware about the specific topic area to understand what products and services are worth recommending to your clients.

- *It is a low-risk, low-effort venture:* While affiliate marketing is not necessarily passive income, it requires very little effort or input on your part. You do not invest any significant amount of time or money on your part.

- *You do not require a support team to be in place:* Affiliate marketing is a very viable prospect, and you can accomplish this strategy all by yourself.

Affiliate marketing can be an excellent source of regular income, but you need to put a couple of things in place first if you want success. If you are just starting out, don't jump into the deep end initially. Focus on launching your blog and getting regular readers then build trust.

However, to be a successful affiliate marketer, you need to be producing regular content on your blog. You need to provide free value to your readers and gain some credibility before asking for sales. You also need to have an email list with at least 500 subscribers. If you can attract and maintain 500 or more subscribers, then you have created a foundation with the potential to earn a passive income.

Some Simple Rules for Success with Affiliate Marketing

Only promote products or services on your blog that you have already used and can recommend your readers. Even if it means purchasing a product to determine its worth, do so to find out if it is something you can recommend. Your reputation will be on the line here so be very careful about the services or products you recommend.

Do not let anyone pressure you into using "black hat" SEO strategies. These are aggressive tactics used to drive traffic to a website. They focus on tricking search engines into ranking them at the top of a search list. Black hat techniques can get you blacklisted and banned from search engine listings.

Never pay any fees to join an affiliate program. You should not even pay any membership or set up fees. Merchants who charge you a fee are often operating a scam on naïve bloggers.

How the Affiliate Marketing Process Works

When you join an affiliate program, you will be issued with a unique ID and a specific URL to use when promoting products on your blog. You will include your unique ID on the link every time you post it on your blog.

Whenever a buyer clicks on the link and visits the merchant's website, the system will identify the customer as originating from your site, and you will be credited with the sale and paid a commission.

How to Choose an Affiliate

1. Choose affiliates based on your readers' interest.

2. Find affiliates that you truly believe in and can respond to questions about

3. Identify a variety of low-paying, high paying, and mid-paying affiliates to diversify the type of income you receive.

Chapter Eight:

Tips, Advice, and Mistakes to Avoid

Here are Some Tips on How to Become a Successful Blogger

- *You need to become a prolific blogger:* The more you write, the better your writing gets. Also, the more blog posts you add to your website, the better you will rank, especially in search engine results.

- *Ensure that you are concise with your message:* People come to your blog for a reason. This is mostly because they want to learn something from you. Learn how to quickly get peoples' attention and how to keep it. Also, avoid fluff and blather.

- *As a blogger, you always have to be analytical:* this means that you have to analyze everything, from your readers' thoughts to statistics, the competition and everything that pertains to your blog and chosen niche. Find out where most of your traffic is from, what kind of posts or headlines attract most viewership and so on.

- *Be a lifelong learner:* As a blogger, learning never ends. If you are a new blogger, then you are probably on a steep learning curve because there is so much to learn. If you want to get ahead of the game and stay ahead, then you need to keep learning because learning never stops.

- *You need to be consistent:* Bloggers need to be focused and consistent. This means that you must be consistent with the topics you choose, your voice and even approach. Top bloggers are also consistent with their timing. If you have regular posting schedules, then your readers will know when to find new content and keep coming back.

- *Successful bloggers need to plan ahead and be persistent:* Success never comes overnight. Real success takes time, so persistence is an essential ingredient. Also, you need to plan ahead. You should know where you are going and where you need to be in a couple of months, a year, and even 5 years.

Here are Some Common Habits of Successful Bloggers

Top bloggers always use Pinterest. It is the best platform any blogger would wish for. Even without a lot of Pinterest followers, you can still send massive traffic to your blog if you pin the right pins. Ensure to include one pin-able image in every blog post. Pin everything including your blog posts, services, products, and freebies.

Successful bloggers will always feature multiple products in their posts. For instance, if you are discussing schools and colleges, do not focus on just one but write a list of the top ten. This is likely to catch the attention of your readers.

Learn to do tasks in bulk if you are to be successful. The term batching simply means doing things in bulk. For instance, if you want to write a blog post, edit it, add social media promotions and so on, you can devote your time to doing one task for a given period of time. You can devote time to perform each task but do it thoroughly rather than perform each task back to back.

You should consistently check in with your email list. Your email list provides you with the best way to share, sell, and promote products and services on your blog. If you are to earn money through your blog, then you should build an email list and keep checking it regularly.

Ensure that you interact and share with your readers and bloggers within your niche. Pros and amateurs are separated by this very notion. If you are to be successful, then always focus on building a sense of community on your blogs and beyond.

At the very least, to be a successful blogger, you must solve your readers' problems. Most of your readers don't care much about what you get up to during the week and so on they visit your blog simply to learn something from you. They need to get advice from you or other similar reasons. If you can solve their problems, then you are well on your way to becoming a successful blogger.

Legal Information for Your Blog

Whether you are a new or seasoned blogger, you need to be aware of legal obligations that pertain to blogging. Apparently, many bloggers get in trouble all the time for what they post.

Journalists and publishers sometimes publish information that other people don't want published. You may, for instance, publish information that someone considers defamatory or a story that is under copyright or even alleged crimes committed by a public figure.

As a blogger, you may not have the benefit of training and resources that can help you maneuver through such complex legal matters. In many cases, the current applicable laws were written for traditional publishers and journalists and courts are at a loss how they should apply to bloggers.

Even then, none of these issues should discourage or stop you from blogging. This is because the first amendment of the US constitution protects free speech. Freedom of speech and expression forms the foundation of any functioning democracy.

However, there are factors that are still legal but not pertaining to freedoms. For instance, issues to do with finances such as taxes need to be considered. Here are some things that you need to know.

Bloggers need to be open when they are paid to promote, use, or review a product. You should be honest with your reviews and endorsements. Therefore, ensure that you explain relationships to your readers.

Blog Disclaimer

It is important to keep your blog legal. As a blogger, you should have an appropriate legal statement on your blog. These statements are there to protect you as a content creator and blogger and to alert your readers about your policies. This helps them view you as a person they can trust.

Disclaimer Information

A blog disclaimer is a short statement that you should include on your blog. It can be a long paragraph on its own page or just a paragraph on your terms and conditions page. You need a blog disclaimer so that others do not rely on the information you put out there and if they do, you are not held responsible.

The disclaimer helps you avoid potential liability. There are no specific things your disclaimer should include. Generally, you just need to ask others not to wholly depend on the information on your blog, and if they do, you cannot be held liable.

Your disclaimer can talk about the nature of your website, the opinionated content, and terms of use. You can include a hold harmless clause which means your content is only for information or entertainment purposes only. You can make it clear that you are not a professional.

Even if you are one, let readers know that you are not providing professional advice but only blogging for information purposes. You need to mention that you reserve the right to change how you run or manage your blog.

- Label information clearly so readers can differentiate between editorial and advertising content.
- Come clean with affiliate relationships. For instance, let your readers know when you have a relationship with a business or company.
- Do not claim to be objective when you are not.

What to do if your content is stolen?

If you create compelling and intriguing content, then someone is bound to take it and use it elsewhere. Sometimes they are unaware they are actually stealing your property. Should that happen to you, simply send them an email and alert them about the copyright infringement. The law protects your content once it is published. Your content includes images, podcasts, videos, links, and original copies. Any honest person will pull down the content. If not, then you reserve the right to sue them and seek legal redress.

Mistakes You Need to Avoid As a Blogger

Many bloggers tend to write very formally. When your writing is too stiff, it tends to put off readers. If you want to draw writers and keep them reading, you need to write in a style that's effortless to read.

Sometimes new bloggers choose topics that are too broad. For instance, you may want to teach people how to do social media marketing or make money online. These topics are too broad. You need to wise up and focus on much smaller niches, then write well and in great detail.

Bloggers will, on occasion, forget or ignore using data as evidence. They tend to make broad statements without backing them up with figures or evidence. A good approach is to always use data. For instance, instead of saying Facebook has many users, you can state there are over 300 million active Facebook accounts. Pointing to reliable data gives the phrase weight and makes it trustworthy.

Conclusion

Thanks for making it through to the end of this book, let's hope it was informative and able to provide you with all of the tools you need to achieve your goals whatever they may be.

The next step is to find a niche that you are passionate about and plan on starting your own blog. It is a simple task, and anyone can manage it with a bit of enthusiasm, passion, and a desire to succeed. There are plenty of people who started blogging on a low budget and are today earning over $10,000 each month.

Do not feel rushed but move at a good pace. Your focus should really be on providing your readers with quality information that is useful and adds value to their lives. Apart from adding articles to your blog, think about adding images and videos as well. These will have a huge impact on your audience, and you will soon be considered an authority in your niche.

All the steps provided in this book have been proven to be effective and can work for you. Work methodically, focus on being consistent, engage your readers, and in no time, success will follow you.

Finally, if you found this book useful in any way, a review on Amazon is always appreciated!

Author Website:

www.julierausch.wix.com/author

Email: Julie@jrpublishinggroup.com

For **Free Offer** please visit:
http://eepurl.com/diLEWT

www.ingramcontent.com/pod-product-compliance
Lightning Source LLC
Chambersburg PA
CBHW030450220526
45464CB00006B/2476